INSIDE YOUR AMAZING
SPIDER-MAN
ANNUAL ...

CAN YOU SPOT THE EIGHT MINI HULKS HIDDEN WITHIN THIS ANNUAL?

WRITE DOWN THE PAGE NUMBERS IN THE SQUARES ABOVE WHEN YOU SPOT ONE OF THE MINI HULKS!

£7.99

INTRODUCING THE AMAZING WALL-CRAWLING, WEB-SLINGING, WISE-CRACKING SUPER HERO...

SPIDER-MAN

THE MAKING OF A SUPER HERO...

THE LIFE OF SHY HIGH SCHOOL STUDENT PETER PARKER, WAS FOREVER CHANGED BY THE BITE OF AN IRRADIATED SPIDER.

YEEOOW!

THE BITE SOMEHOW GAVE PETER AMAZING SPIDER-LIKE POWERS.

POWERS HE USES TO PROTECT THE INNOCENT.

HOWEVER THESE ABILITIES HAVE COME AT A COST.

THAT'S THE THIRD DATE YOU'VE HAD TO CANCEL THIS MONTH!

I'M REALLY SORRY, MJ, BUT -- SOMETHING CAME UP...

AND DR CONNORS TOLD ME YOU FELL ASLEEP IN HIS CLASS AGAIN, PETER...

IF ONLY I COULD TELL HER I WAS UP ALL NIGHT FIGHTING DR OCTOPUS.

BUT REGARDLESS OF THESE PROBLEMS PETER WILL NEVER GIVE UP HIS DUTY TO COMBAT EVIL.

BECAUSE HE KNOWS ALL TOO WELL THE GREAT RESPONSIBILITY THAT COMES WITH THE GREAT POWERS HE HAS BEEN GIVEN!

HERE IT COMES -- OPEN FIRE!
NARGH!
BULLETSSS... CAN'T HURT ME. BUT THE NOISSSE... PAIN...
BLAM
BLAM
BLAM
UH-OH, HE'S COMING STRAIGHT THIS WAY. CAN'T RISK ANY SPIDEY MOVES, THAT'D BE A DEAD GIVEAWAY...
HOSSSTAGE... NEED HOSSSTAGE TO MAKE SHOOTING SSSTOP!
...WHICH LEAVES JUST ONE OPTION...
HONEY, RUN FOR IT! COME ON, LET'S GO!
IT'S NO GOOD, HE'S TOO FAST. NEED TO BUY MJ SOME TIME...
HEY, LEAVE US ALONE, YOU--
UFF!
SMACK

CONTINUED ON PAGE 12

HE MAY WEAR A LAB COAT, BUT THE ONLY RESEARCH **THE LIZARD** IS INTERESTED IN IS HOW TO RIP **SPIDER-MAN** APART! HERE'S THE LOWDOWN ON THIS COLD-BLOODED KILLER!

BLOWN APART!

Once a gifted army surgeon, *Dr Curt Connors'* life was devastated when he lost his right arm after a battlefield blast.

REPTILE RESEARCH

He became obsessed with discovering the secrets of reptilian regeneration in the hope of finding a way to grow a new arm.

MONSTER MUTATION

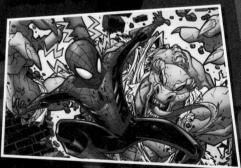

It also turned him into a reptilian monster – a man-lizard with a ruthless and savage personality separate from *Connors'* own!

THE CURE?

Eventually *Connors* created a serum that grew back his arm when he ingested it. But there was just one small side effect...

LIZARD

FACT ATTACK!

The Lizard can whip his tail at speeds of up to 70mph!

He can telepathically control all reptiles less than a mile away from him!

The Lizard is almost as quick as Spidey, and even stronger!

He can re-grow his limbs and tail if they're severed!

Because of his cold-blooded nature, the Lizard becomes weaker in cold temperatures.

The Lizard's ultimate aim is to kill every mammal on earth!

THAT DOES IT. NO BANTER, NO WISE-CRACKS -- I'M ENDING THIS, THE FASTEST WAY POSSIBLE!

SMACK

UNFF!

SLAAAAM

SSSTUPID HUMAN. YOU HAVE BEATEN ME IN THE PASSST BY USSSING CONNORSSS ANTI-SSSERUM -- BUT NEVER IN OPEN COMBAT!

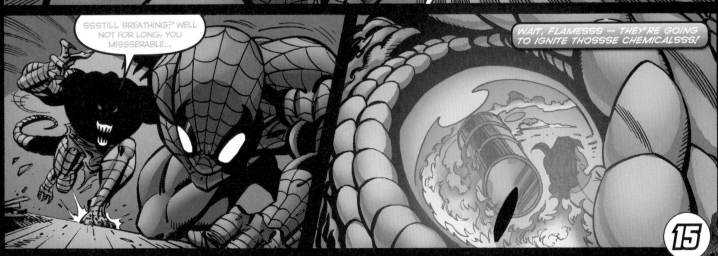

SSSTILL BREATHING? WELL NOT FOR LONG, YOU MISSSERABLE...

WAIT, FLAMESSS -- THEY'RE GOING TO IGNITE THOSSSE CHEMICALSSS!

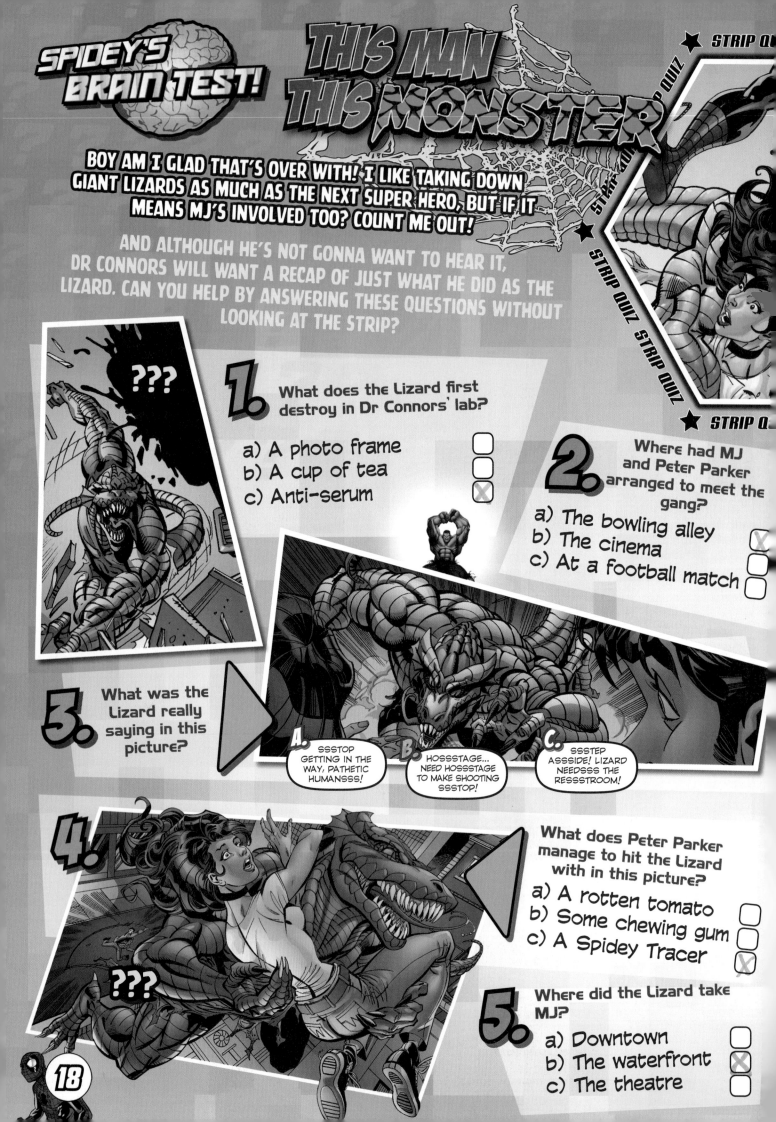

STRIP QUIZ STRIP QUIZ STRIP QUIZ STRIP QUIZ

TRIP QUIZ ★

6.

Can you spot the 4 things in this picture that shouldn't be there?

7.

Who saves MJ from the chemical explosion?

a) The Lizard
b) Spidey
c) A security guard

???

8. SKETCH TEST

See if you can draw this picture of old scaly skin himself, the Lizard!

Copy the image square by square into the empty grid above and then add a splash of colour!

COLOUR GUIDE!

19

ANSWERS ON PAGE 62...

SPECTACULAR SPIDER-MAN

FROM RUSSIA WITH HATE!

SCRIPT: FERG HANDLEY   PENCILS: ANDIE TONG
INKS: KRIS JUSTICE   COLOURS: JAMES OFFREDI
LETTERING: WILL LUCAS

I'VE SEEN MY SHARE OF EVIL OVER THE YEARS. ELECTRO, CARNAGE, THE GREEN GOBLIN -- AND THAT'S JUST YOUR REGULAR, NEW YORK SUPER-VILLAINS!

MOVING UP A DIVISION, I'VE HAD RUN-INS WITH NIGHTMARE, THE RED SKULL, MODOK -- AND LET'S NOT FORGET ABOUT THE MAIN MAN HIMSELF, DOCTOR DOOM. YEP, FOUGHT ALL OF THEM AND SURVIVED...

...BUT THIS TIME, I'M UP AGAINST THE WORST OF THE WORST. SOMETHING SO EVIL, IT DEFIES BELIEF...

...AND THE WAY THINGS ARE GOING, I'M ABOUT FIVE SECONDS AWAY FROM HAVING LETTERS AFTER MY NAME -- AS IN SPIDER-MAN R.I.P.

NEW YORK STATE, EARLIER THAT EVENING...

GOTTA SAY, MARY JANE, IT'S WAY COOL OF YOU TO GIVE UP YOUR SATURDAY NIGHT LIKE THIS. AND YOU'RE SURE YOU WON'T BE BORED?

NO WAY, TIGER. I'VE HEARD THAT JEAN-JEAN OF PARIS IS IN CHARGE OF THE BUFFET...

...AND BESIDES, TONY STARK'S GOING TO BE HERE -- AND HE'S A TOTAL DREAMBOAT!

HEY, WHAT AM I -- CHOPPED LIVER?

ANYHOW, DOWN TO WORK...

...NAMELY, SNAPPING STARK'S LATEST CREATIONS - - A LINE OF NON-LETHAL, ANTI-PERSONNEL ROBOTS, SPECIALLY DESIGNED FOR THE POLICE AND ARMED FORCES...

WOW, PETEY, LOOK - - THEY'VE EVEN GOT A COUPLE OF THOSE THINGS SERVING DRINKS.

YEAH, THAT'S TO SHOW THEY'RE PEOPLE-FRIENDLY. DUNNO WHY THOUGH, MJ, BUT I JUST DON'T TRUST THEM...

KLIK

SOUNDS LIKE SOMEBODY'S BEEN WATCHING TOO MANY B-MOVIES. THE ROBOTS ARE CONTROLLED BY A SECURE WIRELESS SYSTEM, SO THEY'RE PERFECTLY SAFE.

SAY, I RECOGNISE YOU FROM THAT PIECE IN PULSE MAGAZINE. YOU'RE TONY STARK'S PERSONAL ASSISTANT...

OF COURSE, PEPPER POTTS. WELL THIS IS MARY JANE WATSON, MY PERSONAL ASSIST- -

DON'T PUSH IT, PARKER.

YOU TELL HIM, GIRL.

TALK ABOUT OUTNUMBERED! SO I LEAVE THEM TO CHAT WHILE I GET ON WITH THE PHOTOS...

...THEN IT'S TIME FOR TONY S. TO MAKE HIS SPEECH...

...AND ALTHOUGH NOT TOTALLY INVULNERABLE, THE UNITS' ALLOY CASINGS CONTAIN A SMALL AMOUNT OF ADAMUNTIUM, MAKING THEM RESISTANT TO GUNFIRE AND EXPLOSIONS.

21

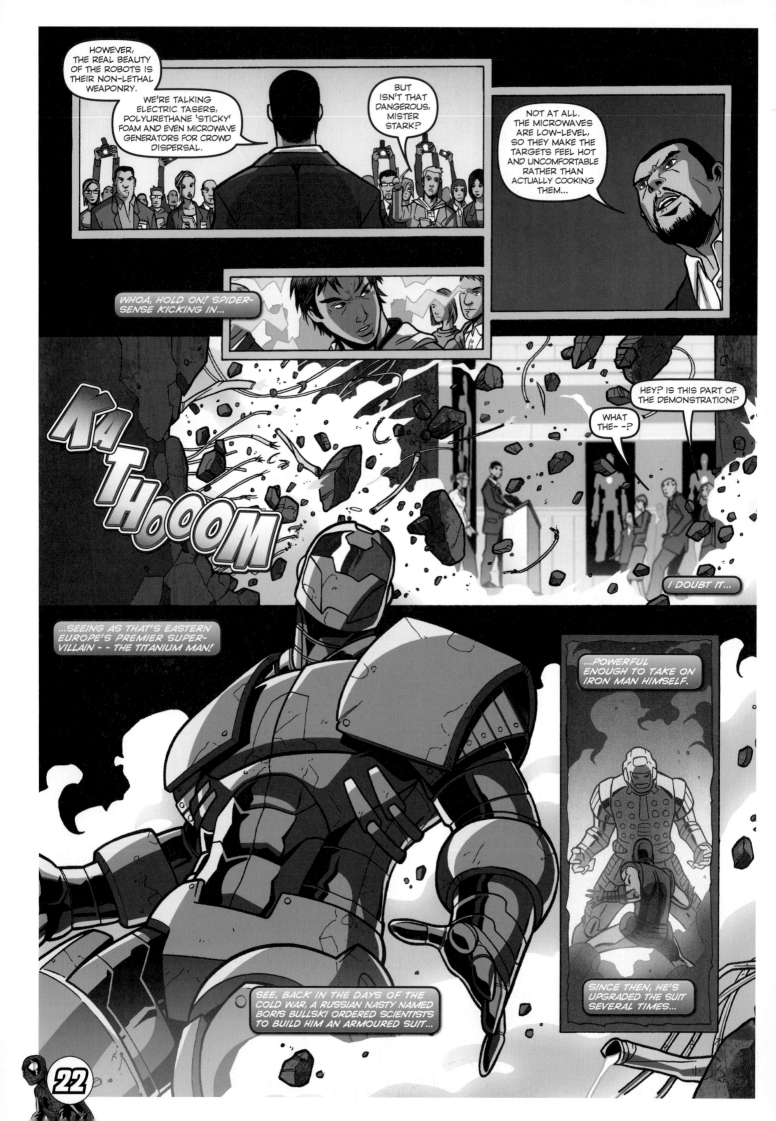

HOWEVER, THE REAL BEAUTY OF THE ROBOTS IS THEIR NON-LETHAL WEAPONRY.

WE'RE TALKING ELECTRIC TASERS, POLYURETHANE 'STICKY' FOAM AND EVEN MICROWAVE GENERATORS FOR CROWD DISPERSAL.

BUT ISN'T THAT DANGEROUS, MISTER STARK?

NOT AT ALL. THE MICROWAVES ARE LOW-LEVEL, SO THEY MAKE THE TARGETS FEEL HOT AND UNCOMFORTABLE RATHER THAN ACTUALLY COOKING THEM...

WHOA, HOLD ON! SPIDER-SENSE KICKING IN...

KaThooom

WHAT THE--?

HEY? IS THIS PART OF THE DEMONSTRATION?

I DOUBT IT...

...SEEING AS THAT'S EASTERN EUROPE'S PREMIER SUPER-VILLAIN -- THE TITANIUM MAN!

...POWERFUL ENOUGH TO TAKE ON IRON MAN HIMSELF.

SINCE THEN, HE'S UPGRADED THE SUIT SEVERAL TIMES...

SEE, BACK IN THE DAYS OF THE COLD WAR, A RUSSIAN NASTY NAMED BORIS BULLSKI ORDERED SCIENTISTS TO BUILD HIM AN ARMOURED SUIT...

CONTINUED ON PAGE 27

COOL, THAT'S THE LAST OF THE ROBO-CHUMPS TAKEN CARE OF...

..WHICH MEANS I CAN HEAD IN AND HELP OUT IRON MAN...

SHOOM

SPIDEY, BE CAREFUL!

RELAX, SHELLHEAD, I'M A BIG BOY NOW!

WOW, I DIDN'T THINK I HIT HIM THAT HARD.

ME NEITHER. NO OFFENCE, SPIDEY, BUT IT NORMALLY TAKES A LOT MORE THAN THAT TO STOP BULLSKI IN HIS TRACKS.

THAT'S WEIRD, HE'S ACTING LIKE HE'S COMING OUT OF A TRANCE OR SOMETHING.

YOU'RE RIGHT. AND I DON'T LIKE IT--

...WHAT IS HAPPENING? WHERE AM I?...

STORY CONTINUES ON PAGE 34 IN THE ULTRON SUPREMACY!

TITANIUM MAN ™

IMPRESSIVE ARMOUR!

Whilst commandant of a remote Russian prison in Siberia, Boris Bullski commissioned a group of captured scientists to build him a hi-tech suit of armour. He planned to use his new battlesuit to impress his superiors by crushing Iron Man.

CLASH OF THE TITANS!

Even though his titanium armour was twice the size and twice as strong as Iron Man's battlesuit, he was still unable to beat him. Bullski's superior officers were furious at his failure, and warned him that he would face dire consequences if he ever returned to Russia!

ROBOTIC REVENGE!

Exiled from the country he loved, Bullski now works as a hired mercenary. However, he still dreams of one day destroying Iron Man, believing that if he succeeds he will be allowed back to Russia a triumphant hero!

His suit makes him powerful enough to lift just over 75 tons!

Titanium Man's original suit was huge compared to his modern armour. Though advances in technology have allowed him to rebuild the suit to be much more streamlined and less clumsy, he is still nowhere near as agile as Iron Man.

Stronger than steel and equipped with a vast array of hi-tech weapons, the Titanium Man is a ruthless mercenary for hire. Read on to find out all about him...

★ SPECIAL MOVES	13
⬭ SPEED	15
✷ INTELIGENCE	12
⚡ STRENGTH	18
✹ DAMAGE	16

VILLAIN RATING

74

He can fly at a top speed of 230 mph.

ARMED & DANGEROUS!

Along with two palm-mounted plasma blasters, Titanium Man also has a number of other offence weapons:

POWER-SAPPER BEAM

– Drains energy from whomever it hits.

MOLECULAR SCRAMBLER

– Capable of disintegrating even the strongest armour.

SHATTER BLAST RAY

– Fires high-powered sonic waves that can shatter any object in its path.

His armour can easily withstand bullet fire, and even shrug off rounds from a bazooka or rocket propelled grenade launcher!

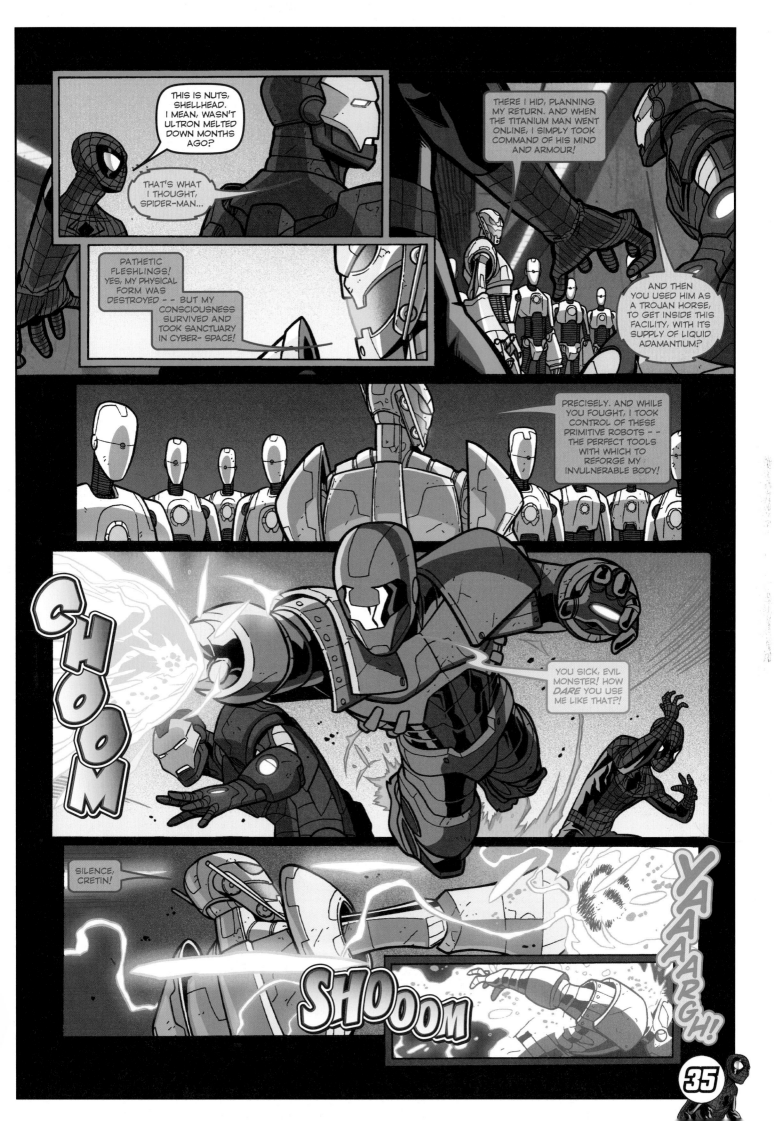

UFF!

THAT LAST BEAM ALMOST TOOK MY HEAD OFF. BUT IF I DON'T DO SOMETHING FAST...

EHP?! MJ AND PEPPER...

ARE YOU TWO *CRAZY?* THIS IS NO PLACE FOR CIVILIANS, SO *SCRAM!*

BUT SPIDEY, PEPPER USED HER SECURITY PASS TO GET INTO THE ARMOURY -- WE'VE BROUGHT THE *VIBRANIUM DISRUPTOR!*

KA-RUNCH

SHIELDS = 55%
POWER CORE: RECHARGING AT 41%

SO, THIS DOOHICKEY COME WITH A USER'S MANUAL?

SPIDEY, GRAB IT -- USE IT TO BUY ME SOME TIME, IT'S OUR ONLY CHANCE!

JUST POINT AND FIRE, SPIDER-MAN, THAT'S ALL I CAN TELL YOU.

MEDDLING FEMALES, YOU WILL REGRET YOUR INTERFERENCE!

SHOOOM

LOOK OUT!!!!

RIGHT, GET BACK TO THE SAFE ROOM. I MEAN IT, LADIES -- MOVE!

OKAY, OKAY, WE'RE GONE! COME ON, MJ!

YOU GOT IT, PARTNER!

NOT QUITE SURE WHAT THE SET-UP IS HERE. BUT VIBRANIUM'S CAPABLE OF BREAKING DOWN MOLECULES, EVEN ADAMANTIUM ONES...

...SO IT'S GOTTA BE WORTH A SHOT...

WELL WHADDYA KNOW, IT'S WORKING -- ULTRON'S STARTING TO LOOK LIKE A POPSICLE IN A HEAT-WAVE...

FWOOOOSH

...GAKK... FOOLISH HUMAN...

...ENGAGING MOLECULAR REARRANGER...

39

CONTINUED ON PAGE 42

SPIDER FILE: ULTRON!

INHUMAN MONSTER!

Ultron is a cruel and cunning android with a robotic brain that only understands one emotion – hatred! He despises all organic life and dreams of a planet ruled over by robots!

MECHANICAL MUTINY!

He was originally created by **Dr Hank Pym** (better known as the super hero **Giant Man**) to be a peaceful servant. Within minutes of being activated, **Ultron** rebelled against his programming and escaped, using his **mind control powers** to make **Dr Pym** forget he had ever invented him!

ENGINE OF DESTRUCTION!

Hidden away, **Ultron** began to redesign his robotic form. After recreating his body four times, with each one being more powerful than the last, **Ultron** finally felt he was powerful enough to begin his war against humanity!

After suffering defeat at their hands on numerous occasions, Ultron has become obsessed with destroying the super hero group the Avengers.

When it comes to psychotic robot super villains, they don't come much worse than Ultron. Read on to find out all bout him!

His adamantium body is so strong it can withstand the force of an atomic bomb!

Built into each of his palms are two powerful concussion blasters!

⬤ SPECIAL MOVES	13
⬤ SPEED	10
⬤ INTELIGENCE	18
⚡ STRENGTH	15
☀ DAMAGE	17

VILLAIN RATING

73

He can lift over 15 tons!

Ultron has a mind-altering Encephalo Beam that can hypnotise his opponents or, at full power, blast them with enough force to wipe their brains!

CONTINUED FROM PAGE 39

...AND BEHOLD -- MY TRUE FORM IS RESTORED!

NOW, SPIDER-MAN, TASTE MY VENGEANCE!!!

ARGH!

NOW YOU KNOW HOW IT FEELS TO HAVE YOUR VERY ATOMS DANCE IN AGONY. BUT FEAR NOT, YOUR MISERY WILL SOON BE OVER!

THAT'S WHERE YOU'RE WRONG, MANIAC...

...BECAUSE THE DISRUPTOR'S SOFTENED YOU UP -- FOR THIS!

ATTABOY, SHELLHEAD -- THAT'S SOME JUICE YOU'RE PACKING!

IT...NGH... OUGHT TO BE. GOT ONLINE AND DIVERTED THE OUTPUT OF EVERY POWER STATION IN THE STATE THROUGH MY ARMOUR...

...AND IF I'M LUCKY...NFF...I MIGHT JUST SURVIVE THE EXPERIENCE!

SPIDEY'S BRAIN TEST!

THE ULTRON™ SUPREMACY!

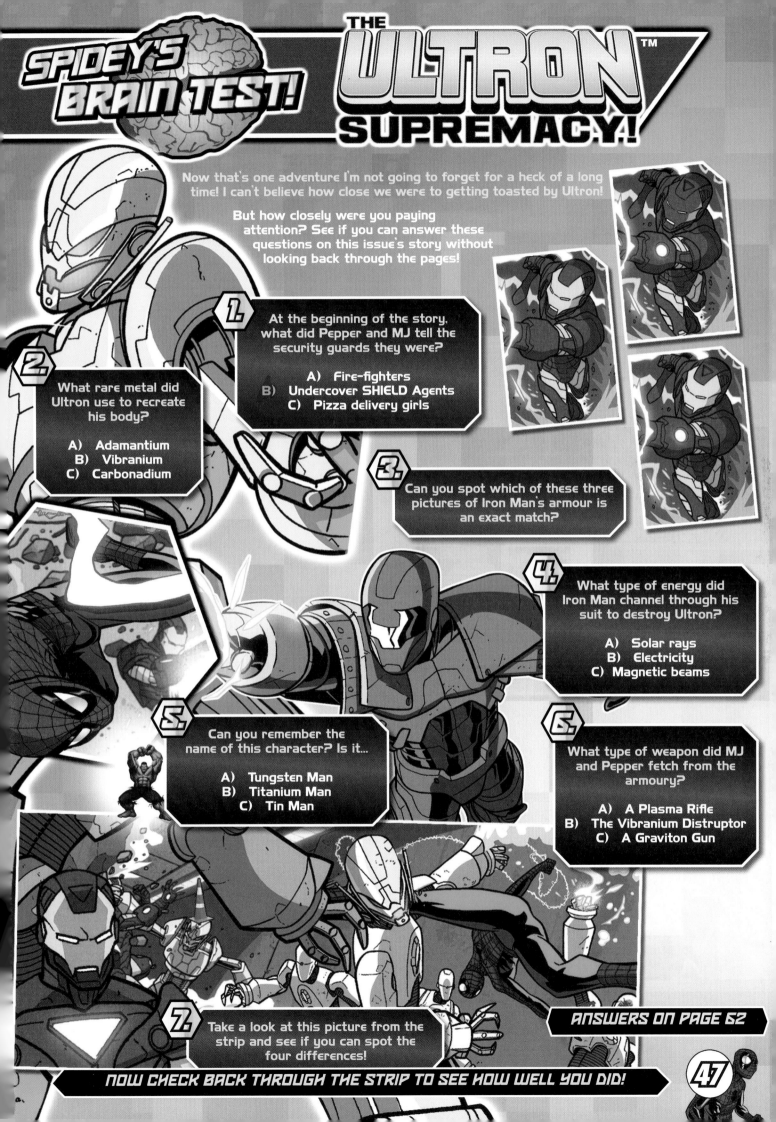

Now that's one adventure I'm not going to forget for a heck of a long time! I can't believe how close we were to getting toasted by Ultron!

But how closely were you paying attention? See if you can answer these questions on this issue's story without looking back through the pages!

1. At the beginning of the story, what did Pepper and MJ tell the security guards they were?

A) Fire-fighters
B) Undercover SHIELD Agents
C) Pizza delivery girls

2. What rare metal did Ultron use to recreate his body?

A) Adamantium
B) Vibranium
C) Carbonadium

3. Can you spot which of these three pictures of Iron Man's armour is an exact match?

4. What type of energy did Iron Man channel through his suit to destroy Ultron?

A) Solar rays
B) Electricity
C) Magnetic beams

5. Can you remember the name of this character? Is it...

A) Tungsten Man
B) Titanium Man
C) Tin Man

6. What type of weapon did MJ and Pepper fetch from the armoury?

A) A Plasma Rifle
B) The Vibranium Distruptor
C) A Graviton Gun

7. Take a look at this picture from the strip and see if you can spot the four differences!

ANSWERS ON PAGE 62

NOW CHECK BACK THROUGH THE STRIP TO SEE HOW WELL YOU DID!

47

HULKBUSTER COMMAND POST ALPHA-ONE. PENNSYLVANIAN AIRSPACE.

GENERAL, I THINK WE'VE LOCATED HIM.

WHAT DO YOU MEAN BY "THINK", SOLDIER? IS IT *BANNER* OR NOT?

AFFIRMATIVE, SIR. GAMMA LEVELS ARE LOW, BUT THE BIOMETRIC SIGNATURE IS A PERFECT MATCH.

ARE YOU *SURE* ABOUT THIS, SIR?

RIGHT, LIEUTENANT, GET YOUR BOYS SUITED UP.

DANGED STRAIGHT I AM!

THAT BLAMED MONSTER MIGHT'VE CHEWED US UP IN THE PAST, BUT THIS LATEST INITIATIVE'S GONNA CHANGE ALL THAT --

OR MY NAME AIN'T *THUNDERBOLT ROSS!*

I'VE HAD WORSE HIDING PLACES THAN A DISUSED BROOKLYN WAREHOUSE. BUT NOT MANY.

STILL, IT'LL HAVE TO DO...

...SEEING AS I WOKE UP THIS MORNING ON THE WATERFRONT -- COLD, WET AND NO IDEA HOW I GOT THERE...

SPIDER-MAN™
GREEN DAY

SCRIPT: FERG HANDLEY   PENCILS: ANDIE TONG   COLOURS: JAMES OFFREDI
INKS: KRIS JUSTICE   LETTERING: WILL LUCAS

...WHICH IS NOTHING UNUSUAL IN THIS CRAZY, MESSED UP LIFE OF MINE.

CAN'T STAY HERE LONG THOUGH. THERE'S OVER EIGHT MILLION PEOPLE IN THIS CITY...

...AND THE LAST THING THEY NEED IS THE SORT OF TROUBLE I BRING ALONG...

HULKBUSTERS IN POSITION, GENERAL.

ROGER THAT, LIEUTENANT, YOU'RE GOOD TO GO.

NO! NOT NOW... NOT HERE!

WE KNOW YOU'RE IN THERE, BANNER. YOU HAVE THIRTY SECONDS TO SURRENDER OR WE'RE DOING THIS THE HARD WAY.

THOSE IDIOTS! THEY KNOW WHAT... HAPPENS... WHEN I... GET STRESSED...!

CONTINUED ON PAGE 55

THE HULK ™

Whilst developing a new experimental weapon for the US Army, Dr Bruce Banner was accidentally exposed to a barrage of unstable Gamma Radiation.

Though he seemed fine at first, the next time he became angry the bomb's true effects became apparent. Bruce's skin began to turn green and his muscles expanded rapidly. Within a few seconds, the mild-mannered scientist had transformed into the HULK!

HULK IS STRONG ENOUGH TO LIFT OVER 100 TONNES!

Bruce now spends his life on the run from the military, searching for a cure for his terrible condition and trying desperately to control the monster within him.

Though many see the Hulk as a monster he has in fact thwarted the plans of many villainous creatures that wished to enslave the Earth!

HULK can floor his opponents by slapping his mighty hands together, creating a powerful sonic boom!

54

THE END

59

SPIDEY

Hey web heads! D'ya think you can help me keep out of the way of the Hulkster's mighty fists by solving these spider-teasers!?

HIDE AND SNEAK!

START!

Spidey needs to reach the Hulk without alerting any of the Hulkbuster units. Can you work out which way he should go to stay out of their way?

FINISH!

MECHANICAL MIMICS!

Only one of the Hulkbuster units below is the real thing, the rest are holographic projections. Help Hulk smash the correct one by spotting which is an exact copy of the original!

A   **B**   **C**   **D**   **ORIGINAL**

CENTRAL!

HERE BE MONSTERS!

A whole load of other Marvel heroes and villains also gained their powers from **Gamma Radiation**. See if you can spot the names of all these **Hulk-wannabes** in the word grid below!

- Harpy
- She-Hulk
- Maestro
- Ravage
- Flux
- Abomination
- Dr Samson
- The Leader

W	A	B	O	M	I	N	A	T	I	O	N	A
D	X	U	L	F	S	M	E	A	D	S	O	C
X	K	R	A	R	N	V	A	Y	P	E	S	D
F	M	A	C	H	I	N	P	E	A	N	M	J
V	O	V	G	N	M	R	H	W	S	T	A	V
T	I	A	S	W	A	P	N	K	X	T	S	Y
A	T	G	T	H	E	L	E	A	D	E	R	W
S	H	E	H	U	L	K	V	H	C	E	D	O

GREEN WITH RAGE

Spidey's managed to snag the **Hulk** with some webbing, but it won't hold him for long! Can you work out which webline has hit him, before the Hulk busts free?

(A)

(D)

61

ANSWERS

SPIDEY'S BRAIN TEST!
THIS MAN THIS MONSTER
PAGES 18-19

1. c) Anti-serum
2. a) The bowling alley
3. B.
4. c) A Spidey Tracer
5. b) The waterfront

6.

7. a) The Lizard

EYE SPIDEY!

MINI HULK!

| 11 | 18 | 26 | 33 |
| 47 | 54 | 58 | 61 |

SPIDEY'S BRAIN TEST!
THE ULTRON SUPREMACY!
PAGE 47

1. B) Undercover SHIELD Agents
2. A) Adamantium
3.
4. B) Electricity
5. B) Titanium Man
6. B) The Vibranium Distruptor

7.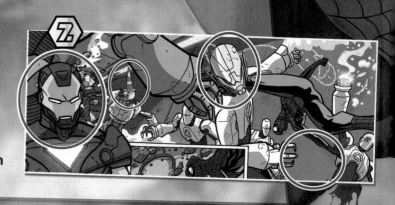

SPIDEY CENTRAL!
PAGES 60-61

MECHANICAL MIMICS! (C)

GREEN WITH RAGE (D)

HIDE AND SNEAK!

HERE BE MONSTERS!